CITIZEN OF NEW SALEM

WORKS BY PAUL HORGAN

NOVELS

The Fault of Angels
No Quarter Given
Main Line West
A Lamp on the Plains

Far from Cibola
The Habit of Empire
The Common Heart
Give Me Possession

A Distant Trumpet

SHORTER FICTION

The Return of the Weed
Figures in a Landscape
The Devil in the Desert

One Red Rose for Christmas
The Saintmaker's Christmas Eve
Humble Powers

HISTORY AND BELLES-LETTRES

Men of Arms (*juvenile*)   From the Royal City
New Mexico's Own Chronicle (*with Maurice Garland Fulton*)
        Biographical Introductions to Volumes I and II of
Diary and Letters of Josiah Gregg (*edited by Maurice Garland Fulton*)
Great River: The Rio Grande in North American History
    Volume One: Indians and Spain
    Volume Two: Mexico and the United States
The Centuries of Santa Fe   Rome Eternal
                Citizen of New Salem

CITIZEN

New York

Paul Horgan

OF **NEW SALEM**

ILLUSTRATIONS BY
Douglas Gorsline

FARRAR, STRAUS AND CUDAHY

to

ALLAN NEVINS

1

HE *assured those with whom he came in contact* [wrote a
friend later] *that he was a piece of floating driftwood;
that after a winter of deep snow, he had come down the
river with the freshet; borne along by the swelling waters,
and aimlessly floating about, he had accidentally lodged
at New Salem. . . .*

The previous winter saw "the celebrated deep snow
of Illinois," as he called it long afterward. On Christmas
day in 1830 came the snow upon all the great prairie, and
snow fell almost continuously in the whole winter. Travellers, if they went at all, went in peril of it. Deep drifts
locked families in their cabins for days and weeks.
In the woods the snow under the trees rose to four feet.

Out on the prairies snow drifts swept up to fifteen feet, and level snow buried all but the tops of last year's corn shucks. The cold held on at ten to twenty degrees below zero. Cattle died. Game—deer and turkey—in their bounteous numbers were all but exterminated. Wolves survived but thinly. Late in winter on a snow blanket six feet deep rain fell and made ice. In their snow-shut cabins settlers subsisted through the winter on little else but pounded meal and boiled corn.

So thick a winter made a flooded spring. The thaw ran over fields making lakes. Roads vanished. The rivers received the melt and rose up until they flowed into the branches of bankside trees. Travellers went by river, in home-fashioned boats. A certain merchant enterprise began when a tall flatboatman with two companions set out from Decatur, Illinois, for Springfield in a home-made cottonwood canoe. On Spring Creek near Springfield they set to work building a flatboat destined for New Orleans. For four weeks they worked until they had a barge eighty

feet long and eighteen feet wide. At night they camped on the creek shore and played seven up. The tall flatboatman did most of the cooking, though occasionally at noon they all went to Caleb Carman's nearby cabin for dinner.

The flatboat was ready in mid-April and with the owner, Denton Offutt, on board with the others, took to the Sangamon River heavily loaded with a cargo of "barrel pork, corn and live hogs." The waters were receding. The voyagers wound along the slow unruffled stream until on April nineteenth they came rounding a bay-like bend where a high bluff pointed at the river. At the foot of the bluff was a mill and reaching out from the mill was the miller's dam. Running to ride over it, the flatboat hung itself up on the dam with its bow in the air. Water poured into the shallow deck. For a day and a night the boat could not move.

It was a sight to see, and from the village of New Salem up on the bluff people came to watch what would happen next. They saw the tallest flatboatman take

charge, though he was the youngest. Giving thought to the problem, he ordered the boat lightened by the putting ashore of part of her cargo. Another part he moved forward, to balance the boat on the dam crest.

Still weighted with water aboard, it could not move.

The flatboatman went ashore and borrowed an augur. Returning to his boat, he bored a hole in the suspended bow. The shipped water poured out. He then plugged the hole and the boat was edged off the dam into free water. It was then a simple matter to stow the cargo again.

The watchers marvelled, and Offutt, the owner, was so taken by the ingenuity of his tall flatboatman that he vowed to build a steamboat for the Sangamon River with rollers under the hull for shoals and dams, and runners for ice, and he would make the flatboatman her captain, and then, he said, "By thunder, she'd have to go!"

They saw the flatboatman dressed in trousers of blue jean rolled up any which way, showing a lot of shank, and a white and blue striped cotton shirt, and a buckeye chip hat not worth twelve and a half cents. He described himself as "a strange, friendless, uneducated, penniless boy, working on a flat boat—at ten dollars a month." The flatboat went with the Sangamon River into the Illinois, and with the Illinois into the Mississippi, and all the way to New Orleans, where selling the cargo the boatmen saw the sights. Denton Offutt remembered New Salem. He could establish a store there in that thriving village on the long bluff above the Sangamon. To help him he hired the tall flatboatman, who had nothing else to do, and nowhere else to go.

2

THE *flatboatman* [as he declared in a sketch of his own life long later, written in the third person] *stopped indefinitely, and, for the first time, as it were, by himself, at New Salem . . . This was in July, 1831. Here he rapidly made acquaintances and friends. . . .*

They knew him better than he knew them, at first, for they recognized the young boatman—he was twenty-two —who had worked the barge off the dam in May, who now had come to remain. He met the two owners of the saw and grist mill and the dam, who founded the village three years ago. One was an ordained minister and the other was the town's first innkeeper, John M. Camron and James Rutledge. A mill, a general store, and a "grocery"

13

(by which was meant a saloon) must be a town's first enterprises. Samuel Hill and John McNeil set up a store in 1829 and when the flatboatman came to stay, it was already the center of village life. William Clary was in business with his grocery and he also ran a ferry across the Sangamon, for travellers who came through the woods to the river. A few years ago, only hunters and trappers came that way travelling alone and vanishing. Later came emigrant parties destined westward who did not linger. But now with farms on the prairies the village was wanted as a trading post. Its lots, laid out by the surveyor Reuben Harrison in 1829, sold for as much as ten dollars, and to put up a log house took as much again.

Now came a man, and now another, and another, each with his skill, to meet needs felt by all. So the village grew. Samuel Hill served as postmaster. In 1830 the cooper Henry Onstot came to live, and two more store-keepers, James and Rowan Herndon. By 1831 there were enough families to attract a doctor of medicine—John Allen, of Vermont. Henry Sinco was constable. Peter Lukins built a house and to it attached a leanto where he followed his cobbler's trade. In another year the flatboat-man would meet the blacksmith and wagonmaker Joshua Miller, and Miller's brother-in-law, Jack Kelso, who carried Shakespeare and Burns in his head. Another doctor came, and Martin Waddell the hatter, and Philemon Morris, the tanner, and Robert Johnson who was a wheelwright and cabinet maker. With them all came their women and their children, and it was not long until new lives were born there, and then New Salem had people who were not strangers. Though some families came and stayed only briefly, moving on farther west in search of their notion of a life, the village at its fullest would have

about twenty-five families occupying twenty-five to thirty
wooden buildings. It was the largest town the flatboatman had ever thought of staying in.

All about lay the prairie under its summer skies, the
color of water as he saw them through gaps in the great
ranks of trees that marked off the open land. Blue heavy
air was caught in deep pockets of the woods, and the air
was silvery above the river, whose water was a muddy
sand color. Coming over the prairie and turning east
you came at a certain point between two creeks that
trifled away toward the Sangamon River, outlining as
they went a high stand of wooded land which pointed to
the river like a finger. Its far end dropped away in the
bluff that backed up the mill. On its flat crest which
curved this way and that the village was strung out in a
long line amid the forest clearings, with prairie behind
it and river before it. Houses were made from the very
trees cut down to give them room. The woods stood close,
with all their animal secrets and good uses and obscure
harms.

The flatboatman saw most kinds of trees but pine and hemlock. He could take fruit from crab-apple, cherry and plum trees, and black and white haw, and gooseberries from bushes. Thick ranks of sunflowers stood up in the summer looking somewhat like the heavy bees that sucked from them. On the forest-edged hillsides grazed cattle, sheep and goats, and hogs snouted in the woods and grunted in the wagon ruts. Small as foxes, and as quick, prairie wolves watched the sheep and took what they could. Every man was a hunter and went for deer and wild turkey in the woods, prairie hens and quail in the open country, wild geese and duck by the river. In spring and summer behind the dam boys and men caught bass, catfish, suckers and sunfish.

A few steps from the village, the flatboatman walked in wilderness; a glance back, and he could see smoke rising from the chimneys in the woods; and standing stock still, he could hear the sounds of life made together by man and nature—the ring of a maul on a steel wedge in a log, and the knock of the cobbler's hammer on leather from Peter Lukins's leanto, and farther along, the cry of the saw down at the mill, and farther yet, an ax in the woods, and still farther, a shot from a hunter's long rifle, and in a silence between all these, if he listened with head turned, the deep booming of the river as it plunged over Rutledge and Camron's dam into the whirl and eddy beneath, where he had first come to notice in New Salem.

As they saw him in his first summer, while he waited for Offutt to come with the stock for the new store, he stood up high in any gathering, for he was already six feet four inches tall, and had been so since his seventeenth year. His clothes made him look even taller, for his breeches—jeans or buckskins—never reached his shoes by

six inches, and his shirtsleeves—tow linen or brown and white checked cotton—hardly touched his wrists, which were as hard-fibered as a thick walnut branch. His hair was thick and dark, coarsely combed, perhaps, by one of his huge hands, perhaps in search of some elusive thought. In his wide-boned face his eyes were set deep in shadow under his strong brows. Bone and long muscle showed frankly everywhere in his frame. He considered himself overly plain, and he seemed conscious of all that he lacked in knowledge, presence and talent. Strength of body he had in plenty; but something in his bearing seemed to say that by itself it was not enough, and that if it were used, it must be used with justice and gentleness. With what could he make his mark, looking as he looked, humbly placed as he was?

A child of the backwoods, he had always held himself less worthy than most. A youth his age saw him in boyhood as "the shyest, most reticent, most uncouth and awkward-appearing, homeliest, and worse dressed of any in the entire crowd." He never put himself forward, and other boys let him look on in silence and take no part in their games—"local contests or pugilistic encounters incident to these gatherings." One day he was bullied by a boy larger than he was and turned to and thrashed him. Thereafter, proved by his physical strength, he was "secured by his prowess." It was not enough. There were other ways to advance. Perhaps he might learn something of these in New Salem village, where he waited for Offutt, and the merchandise, and the opening of the store in a ten dollar cabin near the bluff, and the start of his career as a merchant clerk.

The flatboatman had his first chance to meet people in a crowd on August first, 1831, when an election was held in New Salem. Citizens gathered. He voted for the first time, speaking out his vote, like the others, to the poll clerks who sat at a table. Such a day was given over to politics and pleasure. Men and boys showed what they could do in wrestling matches, fist fights with the crowd as referee, and gander pulls. A potent whisky called Monongahela went around, and rum-like spirits known as tafia, and the stunts grew wilder.

The flatboatman hungered to please.

If he should please them, perhaps the residents would take him in. He could wrestle. When anybody would listen, he could tell a joke or speak a comic poem or imitate an Irishman, a Dutchman, or a Negro, which he could do "perfectly," as T. G. Onstot, the cooper's son, said, adding that "in the role of story-telling I never knew his equal." If to be liked he had to live down his disadvantages, the flatboatman set out to entertain. Caleb Carman at first decided he was "a Green horn," and then he added, "tho after half hours Conversation with him I found Him no Green Horn." So he made people forget what he looked like and come to know how he really was.

It was a trial to be idle. Most men brought their own trades with them to New Salem, and set themselves up to do work for which to be paid in barter or hard money. The flatboatman, waiting for his employer, could only hang around the village, and try to make friends, watching for odd jobs. He earned a little pay for piloting a raft from New Salem to Beardstown on the Illinois River. The raft belonged to a certain Doctor Nelson, who with his goods and family was on his way to Texas. From Beardstown the pilot walked back some seventy miles to New Salem. At least, now, he had a place to go.

The village had no houses of brick or stone. All were

made of logs—white oak, black walnut, or linn—chinked
with native clay. The floors were laid with unplaned
planks. On such a house the roof was pitched, and covered
with clapboards, or shingles called "shakes." One end
wall was almost wholly taken by a fireplace either of
stone, or locally made brick, or wood chinked with clay
(which in a windy day might catch fire). The prevailing
wind in winter blew from west and north, and accordingly
windows were set in south or east walls. Glass for the
earliest cabins came from St. Louis. If a cabin had no
window, the doorway supplied light and air, and these
were regulated by a flap of untanned deerhide or rag
carpet in a hinged frame set in the door.

The interior of the house was dark even in daytime,
for the windows were small, trees arched close overhead,
and the raw logs of the walls weathered with time to a
shadowy ash gray. In summer, transpiration from the
dense greenery so near brought a musty dampness into
the house. Quilting was limp with it, and wood had a
velvety muffled feel. Plaster soaked up dampness. In winter and summer alike, fire was kept in the great hearth. It
brought forth from the heated logs of the walls a pungent

scent which must penetrate the memory and forever bring to mind shelter and protection and closeness to the wild nature which had yielded trees to make houses only a few feet from their source.

Such a cabin was crowded, as the flatboatman saw any time he was asked in. The furniture was strong, plain and sometimes beautiful. It was almost all brought overland from former homes; but as time went by, some was made in New Salem. In a corner was a double bed, dressed with a home-woven coverlet. Trundle beds beneath it fitted the children. Rush seat chairs and a chest of drawers and a corner cupboard and a spinning wheel stood primly out of the way. For a piece of elegance, if it could be had, the family showed a Boston rocker or a Connecticut clock. Beside the hearth was a box for firewood; near the mantle hung tongs, spurs, a bootjack, a candlemold; and over the door and along the walls hung rifles and shotguns on wooden pegs or antlers. Outside, near the door, was a great woodpile which dwindled as winter passed. A rain barrel caught rainwater from the eaves, and at night or dawn after rain the drops broke the stillness with a comforting little song. In back of the cabin was a wooden hopper for leeching wood ashes to yield lye, which went into soap. All about the house grew a garden of wheat, cotton, oats and corn, with a tobacco patch beyond. Sheep belonging to the family grazed in the grass between house and wood. Open to the summer day, the house was a haven of shade and cool; shut to the winter night, a firelit stronghold against the dangers of wilderness and ice. In it the flatboatman saw his present view of home.

3

REFERRING to Denton Offutt, he wrote later that he *contracted with him to act as clerk for him . . . in charge of a store and Mill at New Salem. . . .*

By September second, Offutt was back, paying ten dollars for lot 14 in the village, there to build a store. It was quickly built, and the new clerk went to work. If there was to be any pleasure in business, it had to include a social exchange. The clerk was equal to it. His customers heard many a story, and listened to many a saying, and felt the reach of a mind which made the most of an opportunity for contact with other minds. He seemed ready to help people in any way he could, and now and then he signed as witness to a deed, or wrote out a bond for a friend. He had someone to help him in the store, "Slicky Bill" Greene, who was nineteen.

They had a varied stock of goods to handle. Some of it was imported—dry goods, certain seeds, tools, fire-arms, ammunition, saddles, and fancy liquors. The rest was home-made or gathered about the prairie—cheese, butter, bacon, lard, tallow, hides, furs, mittens, beeswax, hops, vegetables, ox yokes, and raw liquor from a "little still house up at the head of a hollow."

If a variety of needs was posed by such a stock, it made the image, too, of a varied people. New Salem was just big enough to bring together a little world where a man could meet many kinds of men and women, and learn what each might have to teach him about the greater world. The store clerk, in his mild, considering way, seemed eager to learn any lesson in the busy life all about him. Here he saw people use their worth to make a community together. Primitive in aspect, the village in its variety of persons held several of education, grace and culture. The clerk saw a mixed social interest and individual endowment, from the rough body to the quietly cultivated mind. Here was modest opportunity to reach for values of mind and grace. The store clerk, in his own way and time, began to do so.

But first, as a newcomer who hoped to remain, he had to prove himself against the roughest strain of life.

On the prairie near New Salem was a small settlement at Clary's Grove. The "Clary's Grove Boys" paid their respects to newcomers, and the clerk would have his turn. He knew their sort. They ruled in the backwoods with petty terror, hazing drunkards, putting stones or burrs under the saddles of unsuspecting riders, cropping the manes and tails of horses. The Clary's Grove Boys felt free to attack by night the property of anyone who might displease them. They once closed in on a local store, broke the windows, and took possession "of the stock without either ceremony or inventory." By daylight the store was inside out, with its contents stolen or scattered on the ground. The leader was Jack Armstrong. He believed he must take the measure of the new clerk. What he got was his own instead.

Jack issued a challenge to wrestle, since none had ever thrown him. The clerk took him on. They were both good men, in the physical value of the Clary's Grove Boys. It was hard to believe, and accept, but the store clerk wrestled Jack to a draw. They shook hands when they gave up. Jack made it clear to his Boys that the clerk from now on was in good standing, even though he could read, and always had his nose in a book when not otherwise occupied or distracted, and didn't drink, or cuss, or indulge in hazing weaker creatures. The clerk, in fact, found himself in a position of leadership, and though he never interfered with the dissipations of the Boys, he would, on occasion, bring them to be more merciful than they intended to be. They once agreed to give an old drunkard a gallon of whisky if he would let them roll him down hill in a barrel. The store clerk, holding another view of an old drunkard's dignity, prevented the Boys from carrying out the prank. Boxing and wrestling he approved, but if a fist fight flared up out of anger, "Let's stop it," he would say; and they would.

The store clerk saw his customers first in their summer clothes. Many, both men, women and children, went barefoot, and the children often wore only a tow linen shirt. The women wore dresses, tight in the bodice, full in the skirts, of flax, cotton or calico, with cotton kerchiefs, sunbonnets, or straw hats. Like himself, the men wore cotton, flax or tow linen shirts, and breeches of buckskin, tow linen or jean. They kept the summer sky off with plaited hats of wheat straw, rye, or oats. Winter coming, they saw to their shoes. Farmers brought their hides to Philemon Morris to be tanned, and then took the leather and the measurements of the family's feet to Peter Lukins the shoemaker. They could call for the finished shoes in two or three weeks. Some families wore moccasins which could be made at home. In winter, if a man could, he bought a hat of pressed felt at the store, and otherwise, he made out with a cap of raccoon or opossum skins, often with a tail hanging down behind. For winter clothing, the householder took his sacks of wool, pinned with large thorns, to be carded, and then heavy cloth was spun at home, and long coats, full gowns, and for the children little copies of these, stiff and a little too large to fit, dressed the families for weather and society.

The store clerk saw entertainments for play and work and worship. He attended horse races and foot races on Saturday afternoons, and contests of horse trading, boxing, wrestling and marksmanship when men and boys

shot at targets to win portions or all of a beef. Games
and gossip marked election days and trial days, when
the magistrate came to the village to sit. If neighbors
gathered to help another raise his house, or roll the logs
for it from the woods, or organize a wolf hunt, or hold a
quilting bee (when both men and women wielded needle
and thread), every event was reason enough for a party.
And when, hungry for the spirit of God to move within
them, they came together in a religious awakening, as
they said, with shakes and hollers working against hell-
fire and brimstone, then the pleasures of society again
had full cry.

A dance followed every gathering. The furniture was
hauled outdoors, or, if the house had enough room, was
pushed to the walls, and to the sound of accordion, guitar
or fiddle, and clapped hands, the gaunt and formal gaie-
ties of figured dances rocked the puncheon floors into the
dawn. A feast would follow, made by the craft of men
as hunters and women as cooks.

In the open fireplace with kettle, skillet, bread pan and
iron spit, they cooked stews of venison and roasts of
game, pork and fowl; messes of hominy, sweet potatoes,

and greens; pans of corn bread and corn dodgers and mush. All were set forth on board and trestle tables. Preserves were opened for company, and coffee was sweetened with honey or maple sugar. Jugs of Monongahela and tafia went around—the company drank hard. Some guests came from a distance, and needn't think of going back in the dark.

For hospitality was cousin to hardship, and the one-room log house met all occasions. The cooper's son wrote of it: "At meal times it was all kitchen. On rainy days when the neighbors came there to relate their exploits, how many deer and turkey they had killed, it was all sitting room. On Sunday when the young men all dressed up in their jeans, and the young ladies in their best bow dresses, it was all parlor. At night it was all bedroom." And if guests stayed overnight, after the party was over, the bedding was spread on the floor for all to share. They lay down with their feet toward the fire which was kept up all night. Family and visitors slept together, in an unbroken decorum. Women drew off their frocks and men their jackets and shirts and breeches, and hung all these on pegs in the wall. All retained their underclothing and nobody felt "consciousness of impropriety or indelicacy," a citizen declared. If, in the morning, a raw potato poultice for a whisky headache should be needed, any housewife could provide it.

Medical care was largely home-made, though Doctor Allen might be at hand with his Dartmouth learning. Wives treated cold and sore-throat with a piece of peppered fat meat fastened about the neck. To break a fever they set a bag of pounded slippery elm over the eye. If an eruptive disease was slow to break out, they fed a dose of "nanny tea," which was compounded of sheep dung.

Stomach ache they reduced with internal doses of Monongahela and external rubs of cayenne pepper dissolved in
spirits. They gave other remedies made from brimstone,
sulphur, tobacco juice; bitters derived from roots and
barks; and scrapings from pewter spoons. Malarial and
typhoid fevers appeared in the village, and cholera, small-
pox and ague. The ague was so common that people would
say of a victim, that he wasn't sick, he only had "the
ager." If Doctor Allen was called he sometimes had to
accept lard, bacon or dressed hogs in payment of his bill.
These he sold at Beardstown or St. Louis. It was a clumsy
method of making a living, but as the store clerk knew,
no act of life was easy in central Illinois, and an English
traveler said it was "a hard country for women and
cattle." But in New Salem too were love of life and pride
in its extension to a wilderness, and simple joys filled the
heart there as well as anywhere—the sight of a child at
play with a corn cob doll, the homely zest for the tasks
and pleasures of day's end when evenfall brought into
little home-calling windows the glow of wicklight.

The store clerk boarded out with various families, walking to their homes for his meals—the Herndons, the Millers, the Kelsos. At night he slept in the store, and so did Slicky Bill, and their quarters were so close that— a matter of record—"when one turned over the other had to do likewise." Their employer presently rented the mill on the river from Camron and Rutledge, and there, too, he set the store clerk to work, unloading, measuring, and trading for sacks of grain brought in by farmers off the prairie. In mill or store he did his work with good humor, adding many a tall story or memorized joke to his exchanges with customers. Someone noted that he'd rather wait on boys and men than on women and girls, but did not record the reason. He was still shy. Possibly a woman's mind, though no deeper, was quicker than his at trivial concerns. Perhaps he didn't see himself worth offering in marriage. Once waiting on a woman he gave her the wrong change, keeping six and a quarter cents too much. At the day's end, checking over his accounts, he discovered his mistake. He had left a four ounce weight on the scales while weighing out tea. It was an error to be undone by walking six miles with a refund before taking his ease for the night.

In his first winter in town he joined the New Salem Debating Society. The members stirred with anticipated fun when he got up to speak, for his jokes were famous. They were astonished when instead of a droll story he gave them a speech "in splendid style," pulling his hands out of his pockets to fling them about in gangling but eloquent gestures. After the meeting, the president of the society declared that "there was more than wit and fun" in the store clerk's head. "He was already a fine speaker . . . all he lacked was culture." It was a view in which the clerk shared, sometimes hopelessly. But in the following spring, in Offutt's store, using what spare moments he had, he thought he would study grammar. A little while later, he had all the time he wanted for study, when Offutt's enterprises failed. Offutt left town. The clerk was at loose ends. He could find no steady work.

But despite his sober view of his own shortcomings and disadvantages, something stirred deep within him and moved him to give form to a fantastic hope.

In the weeks of February and March he devoted himself to writing a long and earnest statement which he published in the issue of the *Sangamo Journal* for March 15, 1832, announcing his candidacy for the office of assemblyman in the forthcoming session of the Illinois state legislature.

Like other frontier settlements, New Salem and its vicinity felt the stir of the future. Optimists spoke of raising money to build a railroad for Sangamo County, declaring that improved transportation was the key to future growth. The store clerk agreed about transportation, but as for the railroad, "there is always a heart appalling shock," he wrote, "accompanying the account of its cost, which forces us to shrink from our pleasing anticipation." He proposed another measure: "The improvement of Sangamo River is an object much better suited to our infant resources."

He knew the river well—the flatboat, the dam, his work in the mill.

"These circumstances," stated the candidate, "are sufficient evidence, that I have not been very inattentive to the stages of the water," and that therefore his "calculations with regard to the Sangamo, cannot be unfounded in reason."

It was clear from his style that he had been reading the English rhetoricians of the late eighteenth century and in their symmetries of construction he set forth his plan for the river. Though the river had its natural advantages, its course could never be "practically useful to any great extent, without being greatly improved by art." The whole river, he recalled, was clogged by drifted timber, and the last thirty-five miles were the worst, where the channel meandered tortuously. Drifting timber could not pass the bends. Navigation was impossible.

But why not straighten the course "by removing the turf a sufficient width" in a straight line through flat and treeless prairie land, and "damming up the old channel?" The river would "in a short time wash its way through" the new channel, "thereby curtailing the distance, and

increasing the velocity of the current very considerably, while there would be no timber upon the banks to obstruct its navigation in the future." There are also, continued the candidate, "many places above this where the river, in its zig zag course, forms such complete peninsulas, as to be easier cut through at the necks than to remove the obstructions from the bends—which if done would also lessen the distance." He could not say what his measure might cost, but surely it could cost no more than was "common to streams of the same length."

In any case, he believed that "the improvement of the Sangamo River, to be vastly important and highly desirable to the people of the county; and if elected," he declared, "any measure in the legislature having this for its object, which may appear judicious, will merit my

approbation, and shall receive my support.'' By the light
of day under a tree, of a wick at night, the jobless candidate, with no place to sleep but the loft of somebody's
house, set down words meant to sound again in the high
chambers of government.

What he talked about was in the air that spring. Roads
were impassible in spring floods. The *Sangamo Journal*
said that travel by river was ''most eligible,'' and added
rhapsodically that ''the steam boat glides without inter-
ruption from port to port, ascends even the smallest
rivers, and finds her way to places far distant from the
ordinary channels of navigation . . . The *traveller by
water* meets with no delay, while the hapless wight, who
bestrides an ugly nag, is wading through ponds and
quagmires, enjoying the delights of log bridges and
wooden causeways. . . .''

The steamboat, surely, meant the fortune of Sangamo
County. It was immense news, and the candidate heard
it with all others, that Captain Vincent Bogue, of Springfield, intended to bring the steamboat *Talisman* through
the rivers from Cincinnati to Beardstown, New Salem,
and Springfield in March and April, 1832. Captain Bogue
knew the Sangamon was cluttered with floating timber
and overhanging branches. He sent word asking for men
and boys to sweep the channel ahead of him. They were to
bring long-handled axes and report to him at Beardstown. The candidate joined those who responded in high
spirits.

The steamboat would unite New Salem and the county
with the world. The mere rumor of the opening of the
rivers brought new settlers. Towns were laid out along
the streams. Storekeepers already advertised goods to
be imported from the east and south by water. The *Talis-*

man was described as a "splendid, upperdeck cabin
steamer," of 150 tons, 136 feet long, with a 48 foot beam.
Close to the water she had an open fore-deck, extended
in a long bowsprit bearing a staff with a banner showing
her name. Her tall twin black smokestacks rose side by
side from the Texas deck. Her cabins swept in a rising
curve of double decks to the stern. Above her side paddle
wheels her name showed forth again in large letters. She
was painted white. Everyone turned out to see if the
river could take her. Along the banks, men and boys,
some mounted, others afoot, most of them seeing their
first steamboat, cheered and whistled her on her course.
The *Journal* sang on April fifth,

> Illinois suckers, young and raw,
> Were strung along the Sangamo,
> To see a boat come up by steam,
> They surely thought it was a dream.

The ax crew worked at snags and overhangs, and high
water got her safely past the dam at New Salem. She went

on upstream to tie up at Portland Landing, five miles from Springfield.

A public reception and dance followed at the Springfield courthouse. The future had arrived. Captain Bogue had brought it. But meanwhile, the river was changing— the spring freshet had passed, and the Sangamon within a week began to fall to its ordinary low water. The *Talisman* must sail if she would complete her round trip. The candidate was hired as assistant pilot to help Rowan Herndon get her back to Beardstown.

Making about four miles a day, the ship came to New Salem, and was halted by the mill dam, which in low water was an impassable obstacle. The *Talisman* hung on the dam crest.

The dam must be removed.

To this demand of the ship's officers Camron and Rutledge made a furious objection, but the officers reminded them that the Federal Constitution forbade the damming or obstruction of a navigable stream. Navigable? It was now a debatable point. The *Talisman* backed off, threw out her anchor, and her crew tore away enough of the dam to let her pass. Raising steam, she sailed across on the first try and proceeded to Beardstown, leaving behind her instead of proof of a prosperous future a bitter disillusionment.

The candidate and his pilot were each paid forty dollars, and both walked back to New Salem. The *Talisman* sailed on to St. Louis and a few months later went up in flames at her mooring.

4

WHEN *the Black Hawk War of 1832 broke out,* [wrote the candidate, he . . .] *joined a volunteer Company, and to his own surprise, was elected Captain of it—He says he has not still had any success in life which gave him so much satisfaction—*

"Go to the devil, sir!" said the first soldier of New Salem to whom the captain gave an order.

It was one of the Clary's Grove Boys, whose members made up a great part of the company. Despite their free speaking, they followed the captain loyally. The war was a three-month campaign in pursuit of the chief Black Hawk who with five hundred warriors came eastward across the Mississippi in search of food. In doing so he violated a treaty of a year ago. So many Indians on the rove seemed like a threat to settlers. A thousand mounted volunteers joined with regular troops to chase Black Hawk away again.

If the New Salem captain, wearing his calico shirt, knew little of military science and tactics, so with his troopers. He was even better liked when he violated a general order forbidding the discharge of firearms within fifty yards of camp. Placed under arrest, he was deprived of his sword for a day. The Boys gave him their own kind of trouble. One night in camp they took a tomahawk and four buckets, went to the officers' quarters, and stole all they could carry of wines and liquors. By morning they could hardly march. Boy by Boy they fell out of ranks to hold their heads by the wayside. Blameless, the captain was given punishment for the whole company. Once again he was put in arrest, and now was made to carry a wooden sword for two days.

It was, for the captain's company, a war of march and bivouac, without sight of the enemy at any time. The poet and editor William Cullen Bryant, seeking out the front for a glimpse of action, reported how settlers complained that the soldiers "made war upon pigs and chickens." He met the captain, and found much of interest in this "raw youth," with his "quaint and pleasant talk." One of his soldiers remembered his "freedom without familiarity" and his "courtesy without condescension." At an abandoned cabin the company found chickens still scratching about.

"Slay and eat," called someone, and the suggestion was taken up. The chickens were tough. In a while the captain appeared.

"Eating chickens, boys?" he asked.

"Not much, sir," answered a soldier.

"It is much like eating saddle-bags," said the captain, "but I think the stomach can accomplish much today; but what have you got there with the skeletons, George?"

"We did have a sweet jole of a hog, sir, but you are nearly too late for your share."

The soldier offered him the elm-bark dish. Soldiers from other messes drifted up to see what went on. The

captain chewed at the bacon, and then "commenced dividing by mouthfuls" with the visiting troopers.

Easy with his men, he could prevail when he was firm. One day he heard a commotion in camp and went to investigate. He found a throng of angry soldiers clustered around an old Indian who had wandered into the bivouac. He was a spy, they declared, and they would kill him. The old man pulled from his shirt a letter signed by General

Lewis Cass commanding him to white citizens for his good and faithful service to settlers in the past.

"Make an example of him," cried the soldiers. "The letter is a forgery and he is a spy."

They heard another voice.

"It must not be done," said the captain, coming between his men and their victim. The captain's face, as someone said, was "swarthy with resolution and rage." He freed the old Indian to go safely on his way.

By woods and river the campaign proceeded, and the captain's enlistment of thirty days ran out.

"I was out of work," he said to a friend long later, "and there being no danger of more fighting, I could do nothing better than enlist again"—this time for twenty days. Another period of thirty-day service took him to mid-July. In his reënlistments the captain lost his rank and served as a private, like other officers who signed up again after their first hitch.

Late in June, with others of Captain Jacob M. Early's company, he rode up a little hill toward a camp near Kellogg's Grove, Illinois, in the rising sunlight. There they found the remains of a skirmish. The soldiers pulled up in awe when they came upon five white men lying dead.

"The red light of the morning sun," wrote the ex-captain, "was streaming upon them as they lay heads toward us on the ground. And every man had a round, red spot on top of his head, about as big as a dollar where the redskins had taken his scalp. It was frightful, but it was grotesque, and the red sunlight seemed to paint everything all over. I remember that one man had on buckskin breeches."

He helped to bury the five dead men.

The war would end in August with the surrender of Black Hawk. It was an election summer, and soldiers soon returning home talked politics. The ex-captain was still an announced candidate, and the army was a good place to find votes. The Clary's Grove Boys were all for him, and so were many others. Once his willingness was known, "The mess," said one of his companions, "pitched on him as our standard-bearer, and he accepted."

He was mustered out with the rest of Captain Early's company on July tenth, and the march homeward began. The ex-captain had to walk much of the way, for his horse had been stolen the night before. The company was disbanded at Peoria. With a mess-mate, he bought a canoe and started down the Illinois River. The water was low and they hardly made "half the speed of legs on land," said the mess-mate. "In fact we let her float all night and in the morning always found objects still visible that were beside us the previous evening." Coming on a log raft, they were invited aboard to partake of the only warm meal they had for several days—"fish, corn bread, eggs, butter and coffee." At Havana, Illinois, they sold the canoe and set out walking home to New Salem.

5

RETURNING *from the campaign,* [noted the candidate,]
*and encouraged by his great popularity among his im-
mediate neighbors, he, the same year, ran for the Legislature.* . . .

He had less than three weeks' time to campaign for
office. He began by asking the *Sangamo Journal* to make
a public correction in its columns—the paper had omitted
to carry his name in a list of those candidates "who
were on the frontier periling their lives in the service of
their country." His name was now printed as one of the
volunteers—a detail important to a man electioneering

for the first time, though years later he found matter for comedy in his military service, when he said,

"Yes, sir, in the days of the Black Hawk war, I fought, bled, and came away . . . If General Cass went in advance of me picking whortleberries, I guess I surpassed him in charges upon the wild onions. If he saw any live fighting Indians, it was more than I did, but I had a good many bloody struggles with the mosquitoes; and although I never fainted from loss of blood, I can truly say I was often very hungry."

Backwoods citizens gathered to hear the candidates in clearings, where forest trees had been cut down to make an open-air hall. A candidate to be heard jumped up on a tree stump and made his speech—a "stump speech." The ex-captain, now campaigning as a politician, had practiced for it all his life. Even as a youngster, said a playmate, he "would frequently make political speeches to the boys." Though he could have talked only a boy's idea of high-toned argument, he was "always calm, logical and clear." He had taken part in closing day exercises in a school of his boyhood, when the scholars put up outdoors a platform of clean boards and covered it overhead with green boughs and came forth in this leafy forum when all was ready to give "exhibitions" of oratory on such topics as The Relative Merits of the Bee and the Ant; The Difference in Strength Between Wind and Water; and, Which Has the Most Right to Complain— The Indian or the Negro? If as a boy the candidate had ever seen himself speaking in earnest as a man to other men in public, he was able now to make his hope come true. Where it might lead he did not know.

But already he bore inwardly an image of himself which was different from the one that had come with him

to New Salem. An intimate friend said that he had "great individuality which he never sank in the mob. His individuality stood out from the mass of men like a stone cliff over the plains below." If he loomed up naturally because of his physical tallness, he seemed to match it with some tallness of spirit that stood forth on its own account.

Going off to make his first campaign speech he found an audience already gathered for a public sale at Pappsville, eleven miles from Springfield. He wore the dress of his place and time—a mixed jean coat with clawhammer tails which, on him, were too short to sit on, flax and tow linen pantaloons, pot-metal boots, a calico shirt like the one he wore in his Black Hawk command, and "a straw hat, old style, without a band." In national politics he was for Henry Clay, who opposed Andrew Jackson. In local politics, he had already made his proposals known in the *Journal*. At Pappsville, "thar was a large gathering thar," recorded a witness, and "hee was the only canda-date thar and was call on to make a Speach."

This was just the ticket. The candidate got up on a platform or the rear of a wagon and made ready to be-gin. Just then there was a disturbance—one of his friends, Rowan Herndon, was suddenly closed in on by a group of Jesse Dodson's friends. Rowan had licked Jesse not long before and now he was catching it from the gang all at once. He was being badly whipped. The candidate saw unfair advantage. He leaped from his stand and took up a back of the neck and a seat of the pantaloons which be-longed to Rowan Herndon's chief attacker and threw him away a distance of twelve feet. Peace suddenly descended. Rowan Herndon put it that he had been attacked by "a set of Ruggings and they atempted to shoe foul play." Well, sir, the candidate "piched in and Piched them out Like they were Boys and told them his friend Could whip the whole of them one at a time that ended the fus." The crowd got more than it expected. The candidate now re-turned to his rostrum and held up his hand for attention and said,

"Fellow Citizens, I presume you all know who I am—." They did. "I have been solicited by my friends to become a candidate for the Legislature. My politics are short and sweet, like the old woman's dance. I am in favor of a national bank. I am in favor of the internal improvement system''—into which his Sangamon River proposal might fit—''and a high protective tariff. If elected I shall be thankful; if not it will be all the same.''

Presently he made a speech at Island Grove, which pleased his supporters ''though some of the Jackson men tried to make sport of it.'' He made several of his points with the aid of anecdotes, and one of his supporters said that the candidate ''also told the boys several stories which drew them after him.'' These wouldn't bear repeating later in polite surroundings, but there seemed no doubt about their effectiveness at the time. On August fourth the closing rally of the campaign took place in Springfield. The candidate spoke at the Old Court House.

Stephen T. Logan heard him and felt the change of heart which the candidate so often inspired. ''He was a very tall and gawky and rough looking fellow,'' said Logan, ''his pantaloons didn't meet his shoes by six inches.'' This bumpkin? An aspirant to public office? ''But after he began speaking I became very much interested in him. He made a very sensible speech.'' Logan came to the rally thinking of him as ''a sort of loafer down there'' at New Salem. True enough, the candidate was out of work. ''But,'' added Logan, ''one thing we very soon learned was that he was immensely popular. . . .''

The election on August showed as much. In his home precinct of New Salem he received 277 out of 300 votes cast *viva voce*. In Sangamo County he totalled 657 votes. For a self-doubting young man who had been there little more than a year it was a good showing—though not quite good enough to elect him. Once again in his short history he had to wonder what to do and where to go.

6

―――――

HE was now without means and out of business, [he wrote,] *but was anxious to remain with his friends who had treated him with so much generosity, expecially as he had nothing elsewhere to go to—*

New Salem wondered too. His friends saw him jobless, penniless and depressed—the jokester turned miserable and anxious. He boarded with the family of Rowan Herndon, the storekeeper, doing odd jobs to pay for his meals. He thought about what to do. Should he learn to be a blacksmith? It was hard work, but when had he ever feared hard work? Yet with his hankering for books and learning, could there be another way to make a living— with his brain instead of with his hands? There was a way, and he considered it dearly, and gave it up—the vocation of attorney at law, for, as he put it, he "rather thought he could not succeed at that without a better education." The backwoods had made him, had given him his limitations, and seemed sure to hold him forever.

But "before long," he declared, "strangely enough, a man offered to sell . . . an old stock of goods; upon credit." It was Rowan Herndon, who sold out his share of a partnership in a store with William F. Berry to his boarder, whom he regarded as a good risk. The boarder gave his note and entered on his position as a storekeeper with Berry in August 1832 in a narrow cabin of square-hewn logs in the middle of New Salem. "They opened as merchants," he remembered, adding, "and he says that was *the* store."

If it had a convivial air about it, the store offered two attractions. Berry was a drinker, and attracted cronies

of like taste. His partner could be counted on for jokes suitable to all occasions and customers. A backwoods emporium was as sociable as it was commercial. The firm carried whisky in bulk and someone observed that Berry drank heavily from this convenient source. As for the other storekeeper, his "application to Shakespeare and Burns was only equalled by Berry's attention to spigot and barrel," and in addition he read Gibbon, and whatever else he could find, when business was slow. He had a roof of his own over his head now, and slept on the store counter at night. His duties were varied—if a loafer, perhaps too deep gone in liquor, let go with profanity in the presence of a lady customer, the storekeeper hauled him outside and thrashed him.

On January fourth in the following year the partners were paid off for service in the Black Hawk War. Pooling their cash, they paid $265 for the stock and premises of a

larger store, and took possession a few days later. Their
new building was the only one in town finished with
planed lumber. It had a pitched roof of shakes and a
leanto in back. At one side stood a log rail for hitching
horses. The new store was much nearer to the river than
the old one. The woods came almost up to it in the rear.
Early in the morning before anyone stirred or smoke
from new-fed fires showed out of chimneys, creatures
ventured from the woods and came among the houses—
cottontails, badgers, foxes, perhaps a deer. Crickets
clicked more slowly with daylight, and bullfrogs spaced
their gulps more widely. The drilling knock of a distant
woodpecker sounded close. With darts of song, birds in
the forest roof made a net of sound over all. Presently a
door opened here, another there, and voices began to
carry along the street of houses, sounding back from the
long screens of trees that enclosed the village on both
sides. When the new daylight was strong enough to read
by in the square board store with its two small windows,
the storekeeper reached for his book.

He was trying to learn by himself what others took
from school and academy. He said that ''the aggregate of
all his schooling did not amount to one year.'' He had
never even been inside a college or academy building,
as he said. His parents before him had known no formal
education. His mother when necessary ''made her
mark,'' and if his father must write his name he did it
''bunglingly.'' At twenty-three, alone in the world, the
storekeeper felt the need to be taught. English grammar
must be his first subject. One day in February, 1833, he
went along the village and down the wooded slope to the
northwest and came to the schoolmaster's place and
found Mentor Graham the schoolmaster at home.

"I have a notion of studying grammar," said the storekeeper. The schoolmaster looked at him and said, "If you expect to be before the public in any capacity, I think it is the best thing you can do."

"If I had a grammar, I would commence now."

The schoolmaster knew of only one grammar book in the village, and that was his own, which he kept in constant use with his pupils in school. But he thought of another which the storekeeper might be able to borrow.

"I know of a grammar at Vance's, about six miles," he said. It was an old copy of *Kirkham's Grammar*. The storekeeper finished his breakfast, as Mentor Graham remembered, "got up and went on foot to Vance's to get the book. He soon came back with it and said he had it. He then turned his inordinate and almost undivided attention to the subject of grammar." The teacher knew a student when he saw one.

To the little forest settlement where the tasks of life were mostly physical, Mentor Graham and his family brought reminders of other values. He was a teacher by vocation. His own joy lay in the life of the mind, and to the children of the village he transmitted the first, simple disciplines and rewards of learning, taking his pay in eggs and butter, skins and sweet potatoes, corn and deer-meat. During his teaching hours he was formally dressed, with a white tall collar, a stock of shining black satin and a black velvet vest. He was clean shaven. When his classroom day was done he would see the smallest children to their own doors along the crest, for during long snows, timber wolves were bolder than usual and pupils must go their way through woods. At home they had work to do with their books, if they remembered what Mr. Graham told them: "Read aloud when you are alone. Put the book away. Write out your statement of what you have read. Did you get all of it? Look and see.''

The hungry-minded storekeeper came to his teacher with a taste for reading already well developed. He was never without a book, walking by the river or through the woods or along the single street. A boy who watched him said that when night came, ''he read by the aid of any friendly light he could find.'' Sometimes he would go to Onstot the cooper's shop and scrape up shavings and other scraps of wood lying about and make a fire, ''and by the light afforded read until far into the night.'' In the store, he took every chance, even for a few minutes at a time, to take up his book and recite from it to himself. If someone came, he put down the book and entertained the customer with business or comedy. Even in company, if the talk lost his interest, he brought out his book from under his arm and spent a few minutes with it, alone in the midst of others; and then, if a spoken word caught him again, he shut the book away and entered again into the concerns of those about him. He was how he was, and unlettered friends let him be so, for his books never seemed to estrange him from the people he knew and loved. What he learned made him more of a companion, not less of one lost to them in superior knowledge. He talked about what he was reading, and Caleb Carman wrote it down that the storekeeper would ''Refer to that Great man Shakespeare allso Lord Byron as being a great men and Burns and of Burns Poems and Lord Nellson as being a Great Admarall and Naval Commander and Adams and Henry Clay Jackson George Washington was the Greatest of them all of them and was his Great favorite.''

American printers took off copies of *Dilworth's*

Speller after the English edition of 1740, and this was the
first book the storekeeper used, long before he came to
New Salem, along with others including *The Kentucky
Preceptor* (1812), in which he could spell out essays on
such topics as Liberty and Slavery, Industry, Haughti-
ness, and Indulgence; Parson Weems's lives of Washington and Francis Marion; Franklin's *Autobiography;*
Plutarch's *Lives;* the *Arabian Nights,* and the Bible. In
New Salem, while he boarded at the table of Jack Kelso,
he heard Jack quote long flights from Shakespeare and
Burns. James Rutledge had a library of twenty-five or
thirty volumes, and the storekeeper dipped into these,
for he lived for a while at the tavern which Rutledge
maintained in the town, sleeping in the loft. There too he
found other books through a new friend, A. Y. Ellis, who
moved up from Springfield bringing novels by Mrs. Lee
Hentz. The works of some of the eighteenth century phi-
losophers had come to New Salem, and the storekeeper
borrowed them—Paine's *Age of Reason, The Ruins* by
Constantine de Volney, something by Voltaire.

During the spring, summer and fall he studied with
Mentor Graham, in whose house he learned not only aca-
demic subjects but something of the amenity of life by
which the Grahams lived. He saw handsome furniture,
like the six-legged cherrywood gateleg table at which his

teacher put him to work. Mrs. Graham did things with
what style could be managed, and he saw how in the
humble roughness of the backwoods surroundings grace
of manner and feeling could be acquired. He came many
an evening to recite his lessons to Graham. From grammar they moved on to mathematics, and Graham did not
find him "anything of a mathematician—especially so
of geometry and trigonometry." But they worked late,
and Graham's daughter said the two of them "frequently
sat up till midnight engrossed in calculations, and only
ceased" when Mrs. Graham sent them out after more firewood to keep up the fire they had forgotten in their shared
absorption.

The grown-up scholar was a thorough student. Someone knew him "to write a proposition in three different
forms in order to state the meaning as clearly and simply
as possible—and to spend half a day doing it." It was an
echo of Graham's method of study.

How could there be enough books to read?

Colonel Matthew Rogers lived across the prairie near
Athens, Illinois, and Mentor Graham knew his private
library. He sent his special student to borrow from the
collection, which included works in rhetoric and grammar, biography, mathematics, theology, history, poetry,
medicine, and *Don Quixote* in three volumes (Exeter,
1827), and *The Roué* (New York, 1828), and *The Art of
War* by Nicholas Machiavel (Albany, 1815), and *Thinks-
To-Myself* (New York, 1812), and the *Bibliotheca Clas-
sica* of Lemprière (New York, 1805), and copies of Niles's
Register, and Lindley Murray's *The English Reader*
(Baltimore, 1827), which the storekeeper said "was the
best school book ever put into the hands of American
youth." His teacher watched him at study and at play,

and said that "his playful hours were pitching quoits, swimming, shooting, telling stories—anecdotes—and not infrequently truth to say 'sitting up to the fair girls of Illinois.' "

But in the main his life was work, and even the teacher noted that "he was so studious he somewhat impaired his health and constitution." Other friends feared he "might bring on a mental derangement." Fearing for him, they thought of his best qualities. Everyone spoke of his honesty and rectitude, and Graham said he was one of "the most *companionable* persons you will ever see in this world." The teacher's pride was pardonable when he spoke of his grown-up student. "I have taught in my life from four to six thousand pupils as a schoolmaster and no one has ever surpassed him in rapidly, quickly and well acquiring the rudiments and rules of English grammar." Pursuing his true interests, the storekeeper devoted most of his time, said Graham, "to the Scriptures, and books on science and to the acquisition of knowledge of men and things." With modest certainty, the schoolmaster said, "I think I may say that he was my scholar and I was his teacher." In the green light of the woods by day, and at night by coppery firelight, the young storekeeper took out of borrowed books what daily experience denied him.

7

REFERRING to himself and his partner Berry in the store, he declared,—*Of course they did nothing but get deeper and deeper in debt.*

In March, 1833, William F. Berry took out a license to sell liquor by the drink in the store, and to operate a tavern. Stage passengers could buy two meals for thirty-seven and a half cents, or a place to sleep for twelve and a half, or a half pint of French brandy for twenty-five, or a pint of rum, peach brandy or Holland gin for eighteen and three-quarters. The store was becoming more of a saloon. Berry's intemperance was a trial. The other partner was lost in his books. "The store winked out," he said, and when it failed, and when Berry died soon after, he was left owing twelve hundred dollars, which was a sum so great in his eyes that he referred to it as "the national debt." Eventually he would pay it all off, interest included.

Once again he had to look to his neighbors for tasks by which to earn bread and a bed. He had more time for books, but these did not make his living for him. At Rutledge's tavern he listened to circuit riding lawyers and other travellers from the world of which he knew nothing. He knew his own terms were coming alive in him —the terms of mind and spirit; but if they should never have their chance to shine, then anyhow he could show what he could do in the more ordinary needs of life in the backwoods. On the rude prairie frontier all was arduous and physical, if life was to go on. Attainment and distinction came mainly from excellence at the hard brute jobs all about. The ex-storekeeper had innate excellence which could show itself in the humble acts common to all. He had come to local notice by his virtues as a flatboatman, a sort of young wilderness master; and at play as a wrestler, jumper, runner. Shining among others, from the start, in their own terms, he knew their kindness when trouble beset him. A boy who grew up watching him said, "His case never became so desperate but a friend came out of the darkness to relieve him."

Why, think what he could do, they said.

Slicky Greene bet a man a fur hat that his storekeeping friend could lift a whisky barrel and drink from the bung. He won his bet when his friend rolled the barrel up on his knees and drank from it so and spat the whisky out. One of the Rutledges saw him take a barrel of whisky "by the chimes and lift it up to his face as if to drink from the bung hole." James Short was there the day he lifted "1000 pounds of shot by main strength." To Rowan Herndon he was "by fare the stoutest man that i ever took hold of i was a mear child in his hands and i Considered myself as good a Man as there was in the Country until he come about i saw him Lift Between 1000 and 1300 lbs of Rock waid in a Box." And when it came to husking corn on the stalk, he could gather two loads to one against James Short who considered himself "very good." They liked how else he used his prodigious strength, too. Mrs. Jack Armstrong said he "would do anything to accommodate anybody." Widows and poor people who needed firewood brought in could count on him. For a boy in bare feet who needed money to buy shoes he split a pile of rails that could be sold. And "My, how he could chop!" said a witness. "His ax would flash and bite into a sugar tree or sycamore, and down it would come. If you heard him fellin' trees in a clearin', you would say there were three men at work the way the trees fell."

If his worries were not concealed from his friends,

still, as one of them saw, "fun and gravity grew on him
alike," and if asked, he would sing one of his favorite
songs. He always liked *De Blue-Tailed Fly*, which he
referred to as "that buzzing song," and Caleb Carman
said he sang "Oald oald Suckey bleuskin" and "Woodpecker tapping on the hollow Beach tree," referring to a
song by Thomas Moore which the poet might have written
in a wood during his visit to the United States:

I knew by the smoke, that so gracefully curl'd
Above the green elms, that a cottage was near,
And I said, "If there's peace to be found in this world,
"A heart that was humble might hope for it here!"

It was noon, and on flowers that languish'd around
In silence reposed the voluptuous bee;
Every leaf was at rest, and I heard not a sound
But the woodpecker tapping the hollow beech-tree.

And, "Here in this lone little wood," I exclaimed
"With a maid who was lovely to soul and to eye,
"Who would blush when I prais'd her, and weep when I blam'd,
"How blest could I live, and how calm could I die!

"By the shade of yon sumach, whose red berry dips
"In the gush of the fountain, how sweet to recline,
"And to know that I sigh'd upon innocent lips,
"Which had never been sigh'd on by any but mine!"

In this, the elevated slang of romantic convention spoke
for the real emotions of those who listened; and pathos
dwelled in their longings for elegance of sentiment amidst
their rude surroundings.

The unemployed storekeeper could take their delight
in another direction, telling long stories like *Cousin*

Sally Dillard, and *Becky Williams' Courtship,* and
The Down Easter and the Bull. A boy who listened
remembered these—"the very titles suggesting the character of the productions." Children were drawn to the
entertainer, and saw in him something of an elder
brother, and felt his simplicity of spirit which could reach
out to them in childlike fondness and equality. They followed him in summer, dressed only in their tow linen
shirts, sometimes barefoot even in winter. It almost
seemed that wherever he went, he had someone's child

along. One of them said he was "a great marble player
. . . kept us small boys running in all directions gathering up the marbles he would scatter." Those lucky enough
to have work to do could give children little time. Children
loved a man who had plenty of time to give them.

But his friends were at work on his behalf. For some
time they had felt dissatisfaction with the conduct of the
post office at New Salem. They made certain recommenda-
tions, and as a result the unemployed storekeeper received the appointment as postmaster on May seventh,
1833, from the Democratic President Andrew Jackson.
The new postmaster was well known as a supporter of the
Whig Henry Clay, but he explained his appointment,
which he promptly accepted, on these grounds—"the
office being too insignificant, to make his politics an objection." Two friends signed his bond of five hundred
dollars, and he had work again.

The mail arrived by stage once a week. If people did
not call for their mail, the postmaster took it to them.
They said "he carried the office around in his hat." A
letter was a folded sheet sealed with wax. There were no
stamps. The postmaster wrote the postal charge in the
upper right corner of the outside where the address was
written, and the recipient paid the postage. A single sheet
cost six cents for the first thirty miles. For an address
thirty to eighty miles away the charge was ten cents, and
twelve and a half cents up to one hundred fifty miles, and
eighteen and three quarters cents up to four hundred
miles, and farther than that, twenty-five cents. Two sheets
cost twice as much, three sheets three times, and thus
forward. The postmaster of New Salem used an old blue
sock in which to keep his postal receipts. His safe was a
wooden chest under the counter.

Once again his work faced him to the public. The post office was a gathering place, like the tavern. Now he had a connection with the world, too, for as postmaster he handled all the newspapers that came to town, and he read them—the *Sangamo Journal* of Springfield, the *Louisville Journal*, the *St. Louis Republican*, the *Cincinnati Gazette*. If this was an unofficial perquisite, it did something to make up for the low pay of the postmaster, which was based on the amount of business going through his blue sock each month, of which his share amounted to between four and six dollars. He had earned twice as much in his first job as a flatboatman two years ago. To earn a little extra he did small tasks as legal clerk for Squire Bowling Green, the local justice of the peace, writing a summons now and then or witnessing a deed. It was a relief when another opportunity came his way.

John Calhoun, the Surveyor of Sangamo County, offered the postmaster the position of deputy surveyor, to cover the vicinity of New Salem. The work would not interfere with the duties of the post office, and would bring a little pay with it. The postmaster accepted, knowing that he must learn the science of surveying in a hurry. All that summer he was still studying with Mentor Graham, and together they took up his problem. Having mastered grammar in three weeks, he now attacked textbooks of surveying—Flint's, Gibson's—and mastered the subject in six. "He procured a compass and chain," as he said, ". . . and went at it.—This procured bread, and kept body and soul together."

Under the laws of Illinois, a public surveyor was paid two dollars and a half for establishing a quarter section of land; and thirty-seven and a half cents apiece for town lots when these numbered fewer than forty. He was al-

69

lowed two dollars a day for travelling expenses while on official business. The deputy surveyor wrote the description of his first recorded survey on January fourteenth, 1834. It covered an eighty acre tract belonging to Russell Godbey, at whose farm he spent the night. "I sold him two buckskins," said the farmer, "well dressed to fox his surveyors pants. Mrs. Armstrong did the foxing"—to keep the briers from tearing his clothes.

Out on the country with his compass and chain, surveying new townships, roads and tracts, he became known to more people, until his name was a household word. With his open-hearted feeling for his fellow beings, and his comedy, and his book learning, he was always a welcome guest. If his appearance made people nudge each other, it also endeared him to them, with his "blue cotton round about coat, stoga shoes, and pale blue casinet pantaloons," with great gaps at waist and ankles, as they saw him. He was capturing more friends, and perhaps future votes, for another election was coming in the summertime, and on April nineteenth, 1834, he published his name in the *Sangamo Journal* as a candidate once again for the legislature.

Before entering upon his campaign in July, he dealt with a matter as postmaster, addressing a letter to George C. Spears.

Mr. Spears

At your request I send you a receipt for the postage on your paper. I am some what surprised at your request. I will however comply with it. The law requires News paper postage to be paid in advance and now that I have waited a full year you choose to wound my feelings by insinuating that unless you get a receipt I will probably make you pay it again.

He signed himself "respectfully," and wrote the required receipt at the bottom of the letter. Small as it was, New Salem held all kinds of people. He soon went before them again as a candidate.

On July nineteenth a rally was held for the "especial benefit of candidates for the legislature" at Andrew Heredith's mill which stood at the head of Lick Creek ten miles northwest of Springfield. For August second, a barbecue was offered at Hill's mill on Sugar Creek a few miles away, and the Springfield paper said all "candidates of every grade, and all the voters of every denomination; are respectfully invited to attend." Rowan Herndon now lived at Island Grove and one day during harvest time his old boarder came there campaigning, for there were some thirty men harvesting in the field and each had a vote in his giving. The candidate "got his dinner," said Herndon, and then went out to see the harvesters. Herndon "gave him an introduction" but without arousing enthusiasm. "The boys said that they could not vote for a man unless he could make a hand."

"Well, boys," said the candidate, "if that is all, I am sure of your votes."

With that he took hold of the cradle, and, said Herndon, "led the way all around with perfect ease. The boys were satisfied, and I don't think he lost a vote in the crowd."

On the electioneering trail during that campaign summer he saw his old comrade in arms of the Black Hawk War, the attorney John T. Stuart, of Springfield. Stuart had encouraged him before, and he did so again, to take up the study of law. The county surveyor had also supported his aspirations to overcome his lack of education and prepare seriously for a legal career. The candidate began to think that he might after all realize the ambition which so long ago as his boyhood had led him to try reading a copy of the statutes of Indiana. He was now hoping once more to be elected to a law-making body. It would be another step forward to find a living in the practice of law. On August fourth he was elected an assemblyman of the Ninth General Assembly of the Legislature of Illinois and was able to record that he received "the highest vote cast for any candidate."

When the time came for him to leave for the state capital at Vandalia, he regarded his appearance and found it wanting. His old clothes would hardly do, but new ones cost money, of which he had little. His friend Coleman Smoot helped him to buy a new suit to wear to Vandalia, where he was going to travel by stagecoach. Before he left, the assemblyman told Caleb Carman to take good care of Susan and Jane, the two cats he played with as kittens. He would hold them on his lap, and compare their heads, and he decided, wrote Caleb, that "Jane had a beter countanance than Susan."

The assemblyman took his seat as one of the fifty-five members of the House of Representatives on December first. Three days later he received an appointment to the Committee on Public Accounts and Expenditures. He began to learn something of the machinery of government, which seemed almost all a member could do in his first term. "At this session," observed a friend, the new assemblyman "was anything but conspicuous." When the Assembly adjourned on February thirteenth, 1835, he returned to New Salem and his duties as postmaster and deputy surveyor. But he brought with him now a resolve to pursue his dearest ambition.

8

IF *you are resolutely determined to make a lawyer of
yourself, the thing is more than half-done already. . . .*

What if there was no one at New Salem to teach him
the law—no one to "read with," as he said? If a man
must do it alone, he could do so. The main thing was to get
the necessary books and read them, and study their prin-
cipal features. What did it matter if New Salem was a
small town which "never had three hundred people living
in it?" All that mattered were the books and his capacity
for understanding them. These would be "just the same"
wherever he might be. Surely his own resolution to succeed must be "more important than any other one
thing?"

The stage fare from New Salem to Springfield was a dollar and a half. The assemblyman rode in a farmer's wagon or walked to Springfield to borrow law books from Attorney Stuart. He went more than once, and one day at an auction he bought a copy of Blackstone's *Commentaries on the Common Law*. Back home it was now the law books—Chitty or Blackstone—which he took everywhere with him. The neighbors saw him and remembered how he studied wherever he could—"in some nook in a store," or at "the foot of a hay-stack," or "sometimes lying on his back, putting his feet up the tree. . . ." They were used to him and let him be, though to an occasional observer he was a sight. Russell Godbey, the farmer, for whom he did odd jobs, found him one day sitting barefoot at the top of a woodpile with a book. It might seem a curious thing for a farm hand to be doing, and the farmer asked,

"What are you reading?"

"I am not reading," replied the farm hand, "I am studying."

"Studying what?"

"Law, sir," said the farm hand with emphasis. Russell Godbey said it was really too much for him, as he looked at the law student, "sitting there proud as Cicero." Going on his way, "Great God Almighty!" exploded Mr. Godbey.

During the spring and summer of 1835 New Salem had its own excitements. Samuel Hill built a carder and storehouse for wool. The carding machine was powered from a treadmill walked by oxen on a tilted wooden wheel with cleats—a late marvel of the mechanic arts. A new sound— the friction of moving wood, the muffled knock of hooves on wood—entered the village day. On August seventeenth at night a tornado came tubing and screaming over the prairie and in its wake Matthew S. Marsh saw fences flat, trees uprooted, and corn beaten down. At daylight he went to put up his fence and saw to his amazement how "two great wolves walked along unconcerned within 50 yards of me." Eight days later at her father's farm northeast of New Salem, after an illness of six weeks, young Anne Rutledge died.

The law student knew her well, as he knew all her family. She was the third of nine children, and as a boarder at her father's New Salem tavern in 1833 he had surely seen her. She was vivacious and pretty, with auburn hair and blue eyes. At quilting bees she was faster than anyone with her needle, and in the other household arts she was accomplished. She would make someone a good wife.

In 1832 she became engaged to a prosperous young farmer and storekeeper who went east to arrange his affairs with a promise to return and marry Miss Rutledge. Time passed while his letters dwindled and finally ceased. She grieved. The law student saw her so, and certain neighbors wondered if he might be ready to fall in love. A few became sure for all their lives that he courted her and that she was prepared to accept him. She hesitated, but at last wrote to break her engagement. No answer came. Torn between desires, she fell ill and within a few weeks was dying of fever. One of her brothers said she kept asking for the law student and at the last she was allowed to be alone with him. A few days later she lost consciousness and on August twenty-fifth she died. They buried her in Concord graveyard.

New Salem sorrowed for Anne. Some said long afterward that the law student sorrowed more than anyone—

that once again they feared for his reason. Slicky Greene reported that when the snows or rains fell, the law student was filled with "indescribable grief" at the thought of how they fell on her small resting place in the country graveyard. His inclination to occasional low spirits seemed to be increased by her death. She used to sing hymns to him. The last one she ever sang was "Vain Man, thy fond pursuits forbear." Sometimes, even where advantage lay, human pursuits seemed futile. Where of advantage there was none, depression could the more easily enter a man. "Woefully abstracted," said a friend, the law student would range along the river and into the woods. Neighbors kept an eye on him especially on "damp, stormy days, under the belief that dark and gloomy weather might produce such a depression of spirits as to induce him to take his own life."

It was one thing to be given "the hypo," as he called it, by fugitive annoyances; quite another to be lost to the whole daily world. Finally he was persuaded to stay for a few weeks with the jolly justice of the peace, Judge Bowling Green, beyond the little hills north of New Salem. Judge Green loved to laugh with all his three hundred pounds. The shape of his belly earned him the nickname of "Pot." He was good for the law student. The ordinary matters of life proceeded. The law student tended the post office, though someone complained that he neglected his duties at this time. He studied. He surveyed a ten-acre lot of timber. He wrote to the Governor of Illinois to endorse an applicant for the post of public auditor. On December seventh, 1835, he was counted present at the opening of a special session of the Assembly in Vandalia. On March twenty-fourth, 1836, his name was

entered on the record of the Sangamon Circuit Court as a man of good moral character. This was the first of three steps leading to the license to practice law. The law student was coming back to himself. Years afterward, Isaac Cogsdale, formerly of New Salem, said he heard him say of Anne Rutledge, "I loved her dearly. . . ."

Throughout the spring he was active as deputy surveyor, but in May he lost his other position when the post office of New Salem was discontinued by the government. The village had ceased to grow—had even begun to decline. Families moved away. A number of them founded the town of Petersburg which the deputy surveyor had laid out in February. Perhaps the future lay elsewhere.

In early summer an old excitement came back in the air, for it was again a campaign year, and the assemblyman announced his stand for reëlection on June thirteenth. "All," he said, should share the privileges of the government "who assist in bearing its burthens." He believed all whites who bore arms and paid taxes should vote, not excluding females—though he could not have imagined women in the army. He declared further that he went for "distributing the proceeds of the sales of the public lands to the several states."

From July fourth, when the campaign opened at Petersburg, to the thirtieth, when it ended at Springfield two days before the election, the candidate toured the district with his rivals. They came to meetings on horseback, riding into a grove in the forenoon, when the opposing candidates took turns speaking until all were done. If a fight broke out that seemed to depart from fair play, the tall candidate from New Salem stepped in to shake the fighters apart. He spoke in groves and on farms, supporting the Whig position. On July twenty-ninth he

spoke at the farm of Isaac Spear, six miles southeast of Springfield, where the campaign would wind up.

Moving on, he rode past the new house of old George Forquer, who was running against him. On top of the house—it was regarded as the finest house in Springfield —he saw, for the first time, a lightning rod.

What a contraption. He never saw the like. It led him to speculate about electrical conduction. It gave him thoughts about the owner.

George Forquer had until recently been a Whig himself, but now he was running as a Democrat, and what was more, as a new Democrat who had been given the post of register of the Land Office at a fine salary—three thousand dollars a year. No wonder he could build a new frame house with a lightning rod on top. It was enough to give a man the hypo. The New Salem candidate rode on to Springfield.

There the next day he took his turn and made his speech. He was the last. When he was done, the crowd began to go. Democratic Land Office Register George Forquer rose to detain the crowd and they turned back to listen.

He was sorry, he said, but of his opponent, who had just spoken, he must say that "the young man would have to be taken down."

The Democrat, as an elderly and prominent man, had much to say and he said it at length, and with every air of superiority. The New Salem candidate stood aside, listening intently and with growing excitement. His chance for rebuttal came, and he took the platform again, made another speech, and ended with this:

"Mr. Forquer commenced his speech by announcing that the young man would have to be taken down. It is for you, citizens, not for me to say whether I am up or down. The gentleman has seen fit to allude to my being a young man; but he forgets that I am older in years than I am in the tricks and trades of politicians. I desire to live, and I desire place and distinction; but I would rather die now, than, like the gentleman, live to see the day that I would change my politics for an office worth three thousand dollars a year, and then feel compelled to erect a lightning rod to protect a guilty conscience from an offended God."

"*Wonderful*," said a witness, the effect of this reply was wonderful, something he would never forget. The public was captivated by it. Two days later, on August first, the young man from New Salem—he was twenty-seven—was reëlected by the highest vote out of the field of seventeen candidates. On December fifth, then, he was present when the Tenth General Assembly of Illinois met in Vandalia.

He came there with his desired goal more clearly in sight, for on September ninth he had applied for a license to practice law in all the courts of the state, and this had been granted to him on the same day. It was the second official step which would lead him to the work he wanted. Only one more remained. But before he could take it, he must serve the Assembly in his elected duty. Because of their height, he and the other eight members of the Sangamo delegation were nicknamed the Long Nine.

In his current term, as in his previous one, the assemblyman met with a wide range of affairs in the bills proposed, the debates which resulted, the hearings which were required, and the disposals made. All these reflected the needs and aspirations, the concerns and the natures of the men and women whose lives they sought to govern for the better.

The assemblyman took part in the vote on such matters as the works of human justice and dignity which appeared in bills on the establishment of circuit courts, and on the powers of justices of the peace, and on legislative procedures, and on the delineation of voting districts and precincts. With his fellow members he voted on the election of the United States Senator. He considered as a committee member the problems inseparable from the disposition of public monies, and with scarcely a half-cent piece in his pocket, he voted on questions of taxation, of banking, and of incorporation of insurance companies and railroads. The Assembly was much occupied with the development of travel and the needs of people coming and going. He considered and helped to decide upon proposals dealing with public roads, toll

bridges, canals, and river navigation. Education was public business, and the assemblyman worked on schools in general and schools for orphans. Much of the common concern had to do with the homely life of work, household and sustenance. He was on the record of legislation covering cattle marks and brands, the regulation of mills and millers, the "Little Bull Law" which meant to govern breeding of cattle but which was repealed as inequitable, the killing of wolves and the determination of bounties therefor, and—an act which reflected with intimacy and compassion the poverty, the need and the terms of the farmer's life—a bill to declare exempt from legal attachment one work horse or a yoke of oxen, so that daily work might continue. The Assembly took account of human trouble, and the assemblyman acted with his associates on bills looking to the relief of debtors, and bills against gaming, and bills regulating the penitentiary.

It was a broad experience of man and man's ways of constantly reshaping himself as a social being. In his first term the assemblyman had been "silent, observant, studious," as a contemporary said. In the new term, he

was, of those his own age and length of service, "the smartest parliamentarian and cunningest 'log-roller.' " These knacks of his enlivened his efforts in the second term to secure the removal of the state capital from Vandalia. Many towns were after the prize, but Springfield was the leader. The assemblyman led the fight and on the last day of February, 1837, he saw the bill he backed win the approval of the majority. On March first he saw another achievement when in the office of the clerk of the Supreme Court of Illinois his name was entered upon the roll of attorneys as a member of the State Bar. It was the third and final qualification toward which he had worked.

Before the term was over on March sixth, the assemblyman, with Dan Stone, his fellow townsman, filed dissent from a resolution adopted by the House. The House resolution went on record against the abolition of slavery. The Sangamo assemblyman and his colleague made a joint statement saying that "the institution of slavery is founded on both injustice and bad policy." In the temper of the time, however, they added that "the promulgation of abolition doctrines tends rather to increase than abate its evils.'' With this moral act, the assemblyman was ready for the adjournment of the House on March sixth.

During this term his self-image found words; for he told Joshua Fry Speed of Springfield that he aimed—it could only be the pinnacle of fame—he aimed at the ''great distinction'' of being known as ''the DeWitt Clinton of Illinois.'' Governor Clinton of New York was dead since 1828, but he was remembered. Six feet tall, of noble proportions, he was known as ''Magnus Apollo.'' Like the assemblyman, he had started his career in the state legislature. He had gone on to become United States senator, mayor of New York City, governor of New York State, father of the Erie Canal, and a champion of public education. Joshua Speed could be excused if he smiled kindly at the hope of anyone to equal such an illustrious record. On March seventh and eighth the assemblyman, in his short clawhammer coat and his hiked up pantaloons, made his way home to New Salem.

He had come there the first time on the heels of a hard winter. This, of 1836–1837, was another such, when weeks

of rain left puddles and snow melted to slush. Suddenly one day came a violent freeze and the countryside was fixed in ice. Chickens and geese were frozen fast to the ground. Travellers, caught by the shift of wind which brought the freeze, were endangered, and some died. Washington Crowder, riding to Springfield, was overtaken by the storm. Coming to a store he tried to dismount, but—as a local account of the marvel said—"was unable to dismount, his overcoat holding him as firmly as though it had been made of sheet iron." He called for help. Two men heard him and came out of the store. They tried to lift him down, but his clothes were frozen to the saddle. They loosened the girth and "then carried man and saddle to the fire and thawed them asunder."

Home again in New Salem, the assemblyman contained a new resolve. It would not be long until he should make it known.

New Salem had been his school, his academy, his college. There he had learned how to use language correctly and beautifully; how to speak and debate in public;

how to study; how to plan towns; how to write laws by reading law; how to live amidst people and how to respect their common concerns and forgive their uncommon ones. There it was he had left the forest and the river, which had also taught him much, and had found the world. Like all others, he had to find out where to look for it, but it was there to be seen, if he would look, in a hamlet in a wood above a river. In all his young life he had worked to overcome disadvantages, and as they enlarged, so did he, in spirit, patience and strength, among his neighbors of New Salem. They had suffered him when he suffered, and laughed for him when he reached for their funny-bones, and allowed him his hopes, and voted for him when he asked them to. As he was, so had New Salem helped to make him.

On April twelfth the Springfield paper carried an announcement that the assemblyman—once a flatboat-man, a store clerk, a militia captain, a candidate, a post-master, a deputy surveyor, a law student, and now a full attorney at law—would, with J. T. Stuart, "practice conjointly in the courts of this Judicial Circuit Office No. 4 Hoffman's Row upstairs."

The resolve made, it was time to go.

On April fifteenth, 1837, he borrowed from Judge Bowling Green a small pony with a worn-out saddle. In the saddle bags he put his copy of Blackstone, a copy of the compiled laws of Illinois for 1833, three volumes of session laws, two small miscellaneous books, and some underclothes. When he mounted the pony his long legs nearly reached the ground. His fortune consisted of about seven dollars in his pocket. A friend declared that "su-perfically he seemed like a farm hand in search of em-ployment." So it was he rode off to Springfield, leaving

New Salem which, in two years, like the store he had once owned with William Berry, would "wink out."

Springfield numbered fewer than a thousand people but it was a lively town and promised, as the new state capital, to be livelier, after the State House was built. Business houses defined the public square, which like all the streets was dust in summer and thick with mud in winter. Street crossings consisted of slabs of wood. A few small brick buildings contained stores and offices, which were furnished with the barest conveniences. Six stores, a merchant's mill for custom work, and three country taverns completed the public buildings. Yet residents could show style. Some went richly dressed in fine carriages. Little luxuries were imported, and gave tone to literary evenings and political dinners. If the frontier was just down the street, cultivated life could be found just indoors.

The new attorney and counsellor at law from New Salem rode into Springfield on April fifteenth and went to the only cabinet-maker in town to inquire for a single bedstead. He then saw the store of Joshua Speed. He tied his pony and unsaddled it and went in, hauling the saddle bags which he threw on the counter. What, he asked, would the mattress and bedding for a single bedstead cost?

Joshua Speed took his slate and pencil and worked out some figures. The total, he stated, would come to seventeen dollars.

"It is probably cheap enough," said the attorney, "but I want to say that, cheap as it is, I have not the money to pay." They looked at each other. "But," he continued, "if you will credit me until Christmas, and my experiment here as a lawyer is a success, I will pay you then." The tone of his voice, thought Speed, was so melancholy that he felt for him. The attorney said, "If I fail in that I will probably never pay you at all."

Speed looked at him and said to himself that he had never seen so gloomy and melancholy a face in his life. He said to him,

"So small a debt seems to affect you so deeply, I think I can suggest a plan by which you will be able to attain your end without incurring any debt. I have a very large room and a very large double bed in it, which you are perfectly willing to share with me if you choose."

"Where is your room?" asked the attorney.

Speed pointed to the stairs leading from the store to his room.

"Upstairs," he said.

The attorney said nothing, threw his saddlebags over his arm, went upstairs and set them on the floor, and at once returned. Speed said his face was "beaming with pleasure and smiles."

"Well, Speed," he exclaimed, "I'm moved."

The satisfaction of this youthful attainment of a momentous stage could not last.

But for now—while still lost in the inexorable future were the circuit and the Congress and the White House and Ford's Theatre and a lodging in the world's heart— it was enough for the former citizen of New Salem.

ACKNOWLEDGEMENT

In HONOR of the centennial of Abraham Lincoln's first inauguration, the Editors of *The Saturday Evening Post* asked me to write this essay in biography devoted to Lincoln's formative years as a young citizen of New Salem, Illinois. It is published as a book by their kind permission.

Searching after substance for this brief chronicle, I found most matter for my purposes in the following works, which I list with gratitude and respect:

ANGLE, PAUL M. *"Here I Have Lived." A History of Lincoln's Springfield, 1821–1865.* 1935.

ANGLE, PAUL M., Editor. *The Lincoln Reader.* 1947.

BASLER, ROY P., Editor. *Abraham Lincoln: His Speeches and Writings.* 1946.

BEVERIDGE, ALBERT J. *Abraham Lincoln, 1809–1858.* 2v. 1928.

DUNCAN, KUNIGUNDE and NICHOLS, D. F., *Mentor Graham, The Man Who Taught Lincoln.* 1944.

HERNDON, WILLIAM H. and WEIK, JESSE W. *Herndon's Life of Lincoln,* with introduction and notes by Paul M. Angle. 1949.

LINCOLN, ABRAHAM. *Collected Works.* 8v. 1953.

MIERS, EARL SCHENCK, Editor-in-Chief. *Lincoln Day by Day. A Chronology.* 1960.

THOMAS, BENJAMIN P. *Abraham Lincoln.* 1952.

THOMAS, BENJAMIN P. *Lincoln's New Salem.* 1954.

WHITNEY, HENRY CLAY. *Life on the Circuit with Lincoln.* Introduction and notes by Paul M. Angle. 1940.

I make grateful acknowledgement also to Robert Bird, of Lincoln College, Lincoln, Illinois; James Hickey, curator of the Lincoln Room in the Illinois State Historical Library; and Stuart Rose.

P. H.